Grace
for
Educators

Messages of Encouragement for Those Called to Work with Youth

Iris Peterson Bryant

Copyright © 2018 Iris Peterson Bryant

Published by Mattie's Seed Publishing
Greensboro, NC

Cover Design by: Iris Peterson Bryant & K&T Graphics

Author Photograph by: Bryan M. Peterson, BMP Photography

Edited by: Critique Editing Service, LLC

No part of this book may be reproduced or transmitted in any form, or by any means whatsoever including electronic, mechanical, photocopying, recording, or otherwise without the prior written permission from the author, except for brief quotations to be used in articles or reviews.

The names of students have been changed, except where noted otherwise.

Scripture quotations marked KJV are from the King James Version, which is public domain.

Scripture quotations marked ASV are from the American Standard Version, which is public domain.

Scripture quotations marked AMP are taken from the Amplified® Bible (AMP), Copyright © 2015 by The Lockman Foundation. Used by permission. www.Lockman.org

Scripture quotations marked NIV are taken from THE HOLY BIBLE, NEW INTERNATIONAL VERSION®, NIV® Copyright © 1973, 1978, 1984, 2011 by Biblica, Inc.® Used by permission. All rights reserved worldwide.

Scripture quotations marked NKJV are taken from the New King James Version®. Copyright © 1982 by Thomas Nelson. Used by permission. All rights reserved.

Scripture quotations marked VOICE are taken from The Voice™. Copyright © 2008 by Ecclesia Bible Society. Used by permission. All rights reserved.

ISBN: 978-099164791-0

Dedication

For every teacher who has had a positive impact on my life.

In loving memory of my teachers who have completed their earthly assignments—their legacies will never be forgotten

Acknowledgments

Thank You, Lord for the gift and the passion You have given to write a message of hope, encouragement, and grace for others. I am honored that You chose to bless me with this gift and I choose to honor You. Thank You for giving me the privilege to speak to the hearts and minds of my fellow educators. I give You praise for this!

Special thanks to the Grace for Educators' Focus Group: Dr. Barbara Armstrong, Farzana Basam, Kenneth Bennett, Lashanda Carver-Moore, Dr. LaChandra Chance-Parker, Debra Cheek, Robbin Cooper, Whitney Cox, Wendy Dixon, Sarah Faison*, Tracey Jackson, Kevin Leake, Michelle Lindsey, Tonja McPhail, Kia Owens, Dr. Shajuana Sellers, Briana Smith*, Angela Whitehead*, and Anitra Wilson. May you always have reminders of the positive impact you make in the lives of children. I appreciate your input and your encouragement as this book became a reality. You make a difference every day and you are important to the children and the adults who are blessed to work with you. Your educational legacy will never be forgotten.

Thanks to my awesome editor, Karen Rodgers of Critique Editing Services. Your patience and encouragement mean more to me than you will ever know. I am so grateful for the opportunity to work with you.

Thanks to Tomi Balogun, Timiel Dewberry, Monique Johnson, and Alyssa Womble for your advice, support, and prayers as I completed this project. I praise God for allowing our paths to cross.

Finally, to my family—I am thankful for the grace period you allowed me to operate in as I worked on this project. Thanks for your feedback and your patience with me. I am blessed and thankful to call you mine!

*denotes current educators who are my former students

Table of Contents

Dedication i

Acknowledgments iii

Table of Contents v

Foreword 1

From My Desk To Yours 3

Grace To Smile 7

Grace to be Humble 10

Grace to be Fair 13

Grace to Handle Difficult Students 17

Grace to be Organized 21

Grace to be Thankful 24

Grace to give Hope 27

The Grace to know Your Why 30

Grace for What Matters Most 34

Abundant Grace 37

A Final Note 41

About the Author 43

Foreword

There are times in life when God allows you to cross paths with someone who you know will impact your life forever. I was privileged to experience that over 30 years ago when I met Iris Peterson Bryant. Even at that young age, she was a source of hope and inspiration to many in our small rural town. It is extremely refreshing to know that those qualities have grown stronger and spread wider over time. As treasured as our personal friendship has been, I am honored to share the friend and encourager that I have known privately with a world that desperately needs her voice.

As a fellow educator, I know firsthand the pressures of being a part of our educational system. We navigate the waters of testing, policies made by external forces, homelessness, underprivileged children and so much more while trying to be an example of hope and resilience to our students. The issue is that we also need hope. We need encouragement. We need strength. I have walked the halls of our hometown high school as both a student and a teacher with Iris, and I can attest that she is a woman of grace whose words will provide those things for us. I know that because her words are His words – God's words. That is exactly what you will find contained within the pages of this book – God's word. The beauty of it is that He has given her an innate ability to apply His word in such a practical way. You will be able to apply what you read to your life immediately.

My prayer as you read *Grace for Educators* is that you will feel as if a dear friend is speaking directly to your heart. May Iris's many years of experience – the challenges and the victories – be a wealth of knowledge for you. May you feel peace and comfort as you let the words of this devotional challenge and grow you. May it give you the strength and courage you need to continue in your faith and in education. May it inspire you to impact your classroom, your school, and your community.

Debra Cheek
Educator,
Durham Public Schools, NC

From My Desk To Yours

My educational journey began in Clinton City Schools in North Carolina. The district provided me with a quality education and afforded me the opportunity to have excellent teachers who made a lasting difference in my life. My teachers at College Street and Butler Avenue Elementary Schools heard me talk about my dream of becoming a teacher and gave me opportunities to serve as a leader in the classroom. The days that I was allowed to work with another student in a lower grade or help a teacher who did not have an assistant propelled me on my educational path.

Upon entering Sampson Middle School, I was able to explore this dream even further and was given the opportunity to write for student publications each year I was there. These opportunities ignited a passion for writing, and for that I am so grateful. I was blessed to be a part of student educational clubs when I entered Clinton High School as a freshman. My calling as a teacher was confirmed during my sophomore year and consequently, that was the year I decided I would choose English as my college major. I made a declaration to my senior English teacher that I would one day teach in her classroom, and by God's grace, I was hired by Clinton High School in 1998 and given the keys to my senior English classroom, Room 911.

The first day that I entered my classroom, reminders of my educational journey surrounded me. My former teachers were now my co-workers, and the halls that I once walked as a student now served as a place for me to monitor student behavior during class transitions.

The teachers of Clinton City Schools gave me the tools I needed to be successful and it is my sincere prayer that they are blessed because of the seeds they sowed. For years I respected and viewed them as more than educators, they were the epitome of who I could become.

I entered the field of education almost twenty years ago because of the positive impact my teachers had in my life. I never considered another profession and I have never regretted accepting this call.

Although I have had days when I celebrated this choice, there were other days when I have needed a boost. Some days I was able to whisper a prayer and God would give me the grace I needed to get through the day. There have been days when God has allowed me to be ministered to by another teacher or even a student.

Several years ago, one of my co-workers, Mrs. Debbie Shuler, asked me to pen this book. As she and I passed in the hallway, I usually laughed as she asked if I had any grace for her that day. She recently retired and on her last day as a teacher at Thomasville High School, I understood that her words were not a joke, but an expressed need from educators daily. Her request led me to poll a group of my educator friends and their concerns and feedback are at the heart of this book.

As I imagine you reading this page, I would love for us to be sitting across from each other, sharing a treat and coffee or tea. I would let you know that my room is a sanctuary and that it is okay for you to confide in me. We would talk about the number of years we have in education and all of the things we have witnessed over the years.

We would cry, laugh, and even pray, and as a result of sharing and fellowshipping with one another, we would be better educators. We would part ways that day knowing we had a new friend who understands the power of the call to teach.

Read this book as you would take medication—as needed. Each message is designed for a specific situation, so you should choose the most relevant devotion for your day.

Teaching is a precious calling and God's grace is necessary for us to be effective in our positions. Grace, God's favor, is essential to our daily walk. My prayer for you is that the grace of our Lord Jesus Christ would be with you as you make a positive impact on the lives that have been entrusted to you.

May your school year be great because of His grace.

> "But he said unto me, 'My grace is sufficient for you, for my power is made perfect in weakness'" (2 Corinthians 12:9, NIV).

Remember, His grace is enough.

Your Fellow Educator,
Iris P. Bryant

Grace To Smile

During my first year of teaching a senior educator told me I wasn't supposed to smile until Christmas. I was told to be tough and not reveal my soft side to the students because they would take advantage of me.

I wanted to keep my smile hidden so I could be perceived as the teacher who was serious and "by the book." However, it was my fear that my attempt to be tough would disguise the essence of my identity.

I did not think of the student who had not seen a smile all day.

I did not think about the power of connection that occurs with a simple smile.

There are times when we receive advice from someone who has good intentions, but it is important that we are true to our core values and realize how critical they are to our success in the classroom. I understood the teacher wanted me to be firm in my classroom, but wasn't it possible to be firm *and* kind?

During one of our faculty meetings, our principal encouraged us to stand at our doors as our students entered the classrooms on the first day. I decided I would stand at my door wearing a smile as I greeted each student. Amazingly, that simple act did wonders on the first day of school. I did not think about how much a smile would put me at ease.

I smiled and realized how effortless that one act was. I was able to smile because there was a joy that I had been given and I desired to share that joy with others.

Today, I choose to greet others with a smile, not because of an administrative directive, but because of the peace I have in my life. My smile is simply an outward manifestation of what has taken place inwardly.

I smile because I want to give my students hope and encouragement when they put forth their best effort.

I smile because God has blessed me with a job that affords me the opportunity to touch the lives of others.

I smile because I care.

Doses of Grace:

"A cheerful heart is good medicine, but a crushed spirit dries up the bones" **(Proverbs 17:22, NIV).**

"Finally, brothers and sisters, whatever is true, whatever is noble, whatever is right, whatever is pure, whatever is lovely, whatever is admirable—if anything is excellent or praiseworthy—think about such things" **(Phil. 4:8, NIV).**

"A happy heart makes the face cheerful, but heartache crushes the spirit" **(Proverbs 15:13, NIV).**

Prayer:

Dear Lord, thank You for the gift of Your presence. Your presence in my life gives me hope and sustains me. I praise You for allowing Your presence to be felt by those I interact with. I honor You because You have replaced my spirit of heaviness with a garment of praise. Thank You for smiling upon my life and for rejoicing over me with song. I will forever praise You. Amen.

Grace to be Humble

I will never forget the day I was brought down a peg or two by a student.

I had returned research papers and to my disappointment, many of the students had committed the sin of plagiarism. Their eyes reflected surprise when they saw the failing grade written in red ink on this major assignment.

Greg Coxum respectfully told me that his paper was documented correctly and that he did give credit to his sources as he should have within the paper.

My ego would not allow me to even take a second look at his paper. I yelled at him and no doubt caused him to feel embarrassed in front of his peers. The bell sounded to end class and Greg asked if he could remain there a few minutes to talk to me.

I agreed and as his classmates were dismissed, he walked over to my desk and handed me his paper along with his note cards.

The reasonable teacher would have taken the items, told the student the work would be re-evaluated, and written him a note to class.

As I looked at the paper, I realized that I was wrong and the student was right. How could I recover from the statement I had made earlier to him and his classmates? I had a choice to make and I needed to make the choice quickly. I could choose to be reasonable or not.

This teacher chose instead to be unreasonable.

I chose to humiliate and not honor.

I chose to remain wrong instead of empowering the student who took a stand for what he knew was right.

Just as I made the wrong decision, I bent to take a seat at my desk and dismiss the student.

Instead of being a source of support, my chair rolled. It rolled back as I sat down.

This unreasonably wrong teacher landed on the floor as her reasonable right student stood over her.

He also had a choice to make in that same instant. He could look at me like the triumphant one in this battle or he could walk away.

He made another choice. He chose to help me. He wanted to ensure I was okay.

Greg is now married with children of his own and I respect him today because of the role he played in my life.

His actions changed me. I no longer felt I had to be right as a teacher. In fact, I have learned that I garner more respect when I admit I am wrong and then move on from there.

My ego takes a back seat when it comes to educating a child. God used Greg to show me His grace, even when I didn't deserve it.

Doses of Grace:

"And whoever exalts himself will be humbled, and he who humbles himself will be exalted" **(Matt. 23:12, NKJV)**.

"Be of the same mind toward one another. Do not set your mind on high things, but associate with the humble. Do not be wise in your own opinion' **(Romans 12: 16, NKJV)**.

'But He gives more grace. Therefore He says: 'God resists the proud, But gives grace to the humble'" **(James 4:6, NKJV)**.

Prayer:

Lord, give me the grace to admit my wrongs and the strength to move on with dignity. Help me to understand that it is not my responsibility to always be right, but it is my responsibility to behave in a manner that will please You. Help me to create a non-threatening atmosphere that will cause students to feel safe, protected, and secure in my presence. Amen.

Grace to be Fair

There it was in plain sight for all to view; a study released from the Yale Child Center peeked into teachers' sometimes-conscious attitudes about student behaviors. The findings "suggest that teachers who care for very young children may judge those kids' behaviors differently based on their race." The results pointed out often teachers are not aware they are making that distinction—implicit bias.

As I look at the unrest that is taking place in our nation, my heart breaks for the children who feel they are always judged as Dr. Martin Luther King Jr. said, "… by the color of "their skin and not by the content of their character."

My heart breaks for the students who long for the teacher who not only looks like them, but also is able to relate to them.

I have had too many conversations with students who have given up because they don't believe they can be successful in a given teacher's classroom. Likewise, I have witnessed too many teachers become so frustrated with students that they not only despise the student's negative behavior, but they also begin to despise the student.

It is easy for students to recognize when a teacher doesn't like them and it is almost impossible to teach a student who has made that startling discovery.

As educators, we are encouraged to be reflective practitioners; however, reflection is not limited to how well we implemented a lesson, we must look inwardly and examine our hearts. We must be brave enough to ask ourselves the difficult question: *Have I directly or indirectly mistreated anyone who is entrusted to my care?*

A former colleague once shared that she struggled academically when she was in elementary school and as a result, she was very sensitive to students who struggled in her class decades later. She had to make a conscious effort to meet the needs of all of her students—not just the ones that she easily identified with.

Our schools are a place of refuge for many of our students. They should not be a place where stereotypes, favoritism, prejudices, and bias become the norm for them.

I will never forget the wisdom nugget I received from my uncle, a longtime Bible teacher. He stated that although it is impossible to treat everyone the same, it is imperative that we treat everyone right.

Daily, we are given the task to provide support for students who are struggling while making sure that students who may not need additional support are given tools that will accelerate or enrich their learning experiences. We are not treating each student the same, but we are treating each student right. Likewise we must use that same skill set when working with students. We cannot allow our classrooms to mimic the culture that has become so prevalent today. Our classrooms cannot be a place of unrest for our students.

We have the responsibility to push our students and encourage them to be their best. At the end of the day we want our students to be better because they crossed our paths.

We must embody Haim Ginott's message, "I've come to a frightening conclusion that I am the decisive element in the classroom. It's my personal approach that creates the climate. It's my daily mood that makes the weather. As a teacher, I possess a tremendous power to make a child's life miserable or joyous. I can be a tool of torture or an instrument of inspiration. I can humiliate or heal. In all situations, it is my response that decides whether a crisis will be escalated or de-escalated and a child humanized or dehumanized."

The choice is ours; however, the consequences of our choice—either good or bad—will be remembered long after we end the lesson.

Toppo, Greg. *"Study: Teachers' 'Implicit Bias' Starts in Preschool." USA Today.* Gannett, 2016. Web. 29 Sept. 2016.

Doses of Grace:

"He who earnestly seeks righteousness and loyalty finds life, righteousness and honor" **(Prov. 21:21, AMP).**

"This is what our Scriptures come to teach: In everything, in every circumstance, do to others as you would have them do to you" **(Matt. 7:12, VOICE).**

"If, however, you are [really] fulfilling the royal law according to the scripture, 'you shall love your neighbor as yourself [that is, if you have an unselfish concern for others and do things for their benefit]' you are doing well" **(James 2:8, AMP).**

Prayer:

Lord, please forgive me for the times that I overlooked, misjudged, mistreated, or harbored misconceptions in my heart toward any of my students. I thank you for being the perfect example of righteousness and I ask for Your help so that I can emulate Your ability to love all people. Help me to see the students as You see them. Help me to love as You love. Help me to teach as You teach—by example, in word and deed. Amen.

Grace to Handle Difficult Students

During my first years as a teacher, our school used the Assertive Discipline Plan for behavioral issues, which we called the "name-check" system. The first time a student misbehaved, his name would be written on the board. If a check was placed beside the name, that student would be assigned to 15 minutes of detention, 30 minutes of detention would be given with the second check, and the third check would warrant a disciplinary referral. I took pride in knowing that most students would self-correct after the second check. During that "era" in education, students and parents frowned upon office referrals.

Then one day, my most memorable student entered my classroom and the "name-check" system was a joke for him. He sat in four different seats within a 45 minute block and decreed that he had never moved from his seat. He had a different name each day, and had no regard for the classroom or school rules. What had I done to deserve this? If ⁺Lee was the only behavioral problem in that class, I would have considered myself blessed; however, there were other students that had behaviors that were difficult to handle.

My initial mistake occurred when I failed to seek assistance from veteran teachers. I wanted to appear to have it all together and I felt that if I asked for help, I would be perceived as weak or ignorant. So, when I talked to my co-workers about Lee I joked and acted like he was not a handful. The truth was I did not even know what assistance I needed to ask for. I flipped through my undergrad books, read and re-read books by educational gurus, and at the end of the year, Lee failed my class. And I had failed Lee.

Today, I serve as a lead mentor and I see teachers daily who remind me of myself during my first years in the classroom. There are many difficult students that need someone to build a positive relationship with them. There are interest inventories that students may complete that could help teachers add things that interest the student to the various lessons. There are some students who come across as difficult, but they simply need to know they have a champion in the building who is cheering them on. If the student is an athlete, form a relationship with the coach to see ways that you can help the student achieve success in your classroom. If the student is not being challenged in your classroom, differentiate your lessons so that he can move on to new material while other students complete a different task.

Lee left my classroom in 2000 and when I saw him enter the classroom across the hall from me on the first day of school the following fall, he was a completely different student.

I followed him to the class and watched him enter in a calm manner. The teacher greeted him and he responded respectfully. Throughout the semester, I dropped in and asked the teacher what happened to my former student. We both laughed because she noticed the change as well. Sometime between the last day of one school year and the first day of another, Lee had matured.

The positive changes that we desire to see in our students may not always occur while they are enrolled in our classes. We may employ all of the strategies and principles that we know and we may not see the results. This should not cause us to give up. We have to know that we are making a difference in the life of the child.

Remember, the gardener plants a seed and expects a great harvest. He nurtures the seed by providing water and sunlight. He does not see the work that occurs underground, but he knows that once the root has developed, the plant will soon emerge.

Likewise, as educators, we must take the time to provide the proper environment for all of our students to become successful. Even if we do not see the fruits of a labor while that student's name is on our roster, we must believe that what one day that student will emerge into the productive citizen that he has the potential to become.

In 2010, I saw Lee in our local grocery store. I spoke to him by name and his first response was, "You remember me?" I laughed because he is a student I will never forget.

Because I didn't get it right with Lee, I am determined that I will get it right with all of the "Lees" that follow.

My focus cannot remain on Lee, but I must focus on me.

Doses of Grace:

> "The Lord appeared to us in the past, saying: 'I have loved you with an everlasting love; I have drawn you with unfailing kindness'" **(Jeremiah 31:3 NIV)**.

> "Dear children, let us not love with words or speech but with actions and in truth" **(I John 3:18, NIV)**.

> "Everyone who believes that Jesus is the Christ is born of God, and everyone who loves the father loves his child as well. This is how we know that we love the children of God: by loving God and carrying out his commands. In fact, this is love for God: to keep his commands" **(1 John 5:1-3a, NIV)**.

Prayer:

Lord, I bring all of the frustration I have in my heart to You and I place it at Your feet. I don't always say the right thing or do the right thing, so help me to listen to Your warnings and submit to Spirit each day. I long to please You in every area of my life, so I seek Your wisdom and Your knowledge, and Your guidance right now. Please settle me so I can speak words that will bring peace to my students. Allow Your strength to overshadow my weaknesses so I will honor You. You have called and equipped me for this assignment. Give me the grace to carry it out in a manner that pleases You.

Grace to be Organized

As my co-worker joked about the piles of papers on my desk and the table next to my desk, I used laughter to disguise my embarrassment. I was ashamed of the area in my room I tried to hide from others, and I didn't feel I could be vulnerable enough to let her know I just didn't know where to start in this quest for organization.

The truth is, although I laughed about her jokes, I desperately wanted my room to be neat and orderly like hers, I just did not know how to make that happen. I was a first year teacher acting like I had been teaching for decades and I believed that asking for help was a sign of weakness.

Those piles on my desk represented the piles I was housing internally. My thoughts were cluttered, my life was in disarray, and I was overextended in every area of my life. My desk was a direct representation of my life and honestly, I did not know where to begin to bring order out of the chaos.

As my co-worker retreated to her orderly room, I was reminded of a conversation I'd had with another educator a few months earlier.

My department chair shared a strategy with me that had been ingrained in her since her days of teaching at a private school decades earlier.

"Do not leave for the day without getting your desk in order." She insisted that this strategy had kept her organized and caused her to begin each day in an organized and orderly manner.

There are countless organizational systems available for purchase, but there are a few practical tips that require little or no financial investment.

- A critical element for getting organized and staying that way is simply knowing what to save and what to toss.
- Make sure every paper has a home.
- Use folders to organize your papers and use bins to organize student work.

Those practices help diminish the need to panic because of a misplaced form, homework assignment, or test.

If you still don't know what to do to restore the order in your classroom, link up with a teacher who is extremely organized and ask them to serve as your accountability partner.

Most importantly, take inventory of your life. Ask God to give you the necessary grace to rid your life of anything that causes clutter and prevents you from effectively operating in the position that He has called you into. My pastor teaches us that the spiritual principle of organization is God's plan to simplify our lives.

Being organized today can save you from headache tomorrow. Operating decently and orderly begins within us.

Doses of Grace:

> "Let all things be done decently and in order" **(1 Corinthians 14:40, NKJV).**

> "Whatever you do [whatever your task may be], work from the soul [that is, put in your very best effort], as [something done] for the Lord and not for men" **(Col. 3:23, AMP).**

> "For God is not a God of confusion, but of peace" **(1 Corinthians 14:33, ASV).**

Prayer:

Lord, please give me the peace and order internally so I can demonstrate peace and order externally. Help me to understand priority and the power of the word no. Allow me to understand that in order for my life to be simplified, I must operate from a standpoint of order and organization. Guide me as I prioritize my educational life so I can operate in a place of harmony and not discord. Your will. Your plan. Your way. Amen.

Grace to be Thankful

During one of my most stressful years as an educator, I had the privilege of meeting a woman who shifted my perspective on gratitude.

One of my co-workers invited an international guest speaker to our school. As I accompanied my students to the Media Center for her presentation, I was not prepared for the impact her message would have on me.

She offered words of encouragement, but when she allowed us to peek into her heart I was able to see much more than what she presented to our students. She spoke with tear-filled eyes as she described the things she'd witnessed during a visit to a local fast food restaurant. The extreme waste she witnessed saddened her. She cried as she described her feelings watching people toss food in the garbage. I had witnessed the same thing too—in restaurants, the school cafeteria, and even my home.

As I thought about the things I throw away, I felt a pang of guilt for the times I did not show gratitude and the countless times I took my everyday provisions for granted.

I had just complained about my classroom being too cold, but I failed to offer thanks for teaching in a building that was structurally sound.

My mind went back to the day another student was added to my overflowing classroom. Instead of complaining, I should have offered thanks that I had a classroom that was safe and welcoming to all students.

I had complained on my last pay day because there were things I wanted to do, but I paused that morning to give thanks because all of my needs were met.

In spite of the things I sometimes viewed as a deficiency, I paused and offered thanks for having all sufficiency in all things.

No matter how bad things appeared to be, our speaker reminded us the students who lived in her country would be grateful to have the things we were complaining about.

That moment in the Media Center, I turned my heart to God and repented for the times I had taken His bountiful blessings for granted. I thought of my students who seemed as captivated by her presentation as I was. I prayed for them and I offered thanks that God entrusted each one of them into my care.

While having a moment to reflect, I prayed that I would never require harsh nudges to remind me of how much my Father has blessed me. I want to live each day with an attitude of gratitude and a heart of thanksgiving. There is someone, somewhere who prays earnestly for the multitude of things I take for granted.

Doses of Grace:

"Enter into his gates with thanksgiving, and into his courts with praise: be thankful unto him, and bless his name" **(Psalm 100:4, KJV).**

"Let us come before his presence with thanksgiving, and make a joyful noise unto him with psalms" **(Psalm 95:2, KJV).**

"Do not be anxious *or* worried about anything, but in everything [every circumstance and situation] by prayer and petition with thanksgiving, continue to make your [specific] requests known to God" **(Philippians 4:6, AMP).**

Prayer:

Please help me Lord to be a ray of light to my students who may not have everything they need. Allow my attitude to be one of gratefulness at all times. Help me to trust You to meet all of needs—in the classroom and beyond. Thank You for choosing me to carry out this assignment. Thank You for equipping me with the grace needed to demonstrate a lifestyle of gratefulness.

Grace to give Hope

One of my former administrators shared this story about building relationships with students.

During the administrator's time as a teacher, a student, [+]Kim, entered her math class with a huge chip on her shoulder. She behaved as if the world owed her everything and she was quick to discuss her upbringing and how it contributed to her outlook on life.

She believed that her address dictated her destiny.

The teacher was offended by her attitude and her actions. She was frustrated because the student did not believe she would ever have a life better than the one she was living. The teacher refused to accept the low expectations from the student because her upbringing mirrored that of her student.

One day the teacher asked Kim to remain after class for a moment.

Kim had heard about her teacher's home life when she was in high school. She learned that her teacher spent more time with her grandmother than she spent with her mother because of the many struggles and battles that her mother had to fight.

The administrator indicated to me that Kim's demeanor changed, not because she felt the teacher understood her, but because she viewed her teacher as a success story.

We are not always afforded the opportunity to have a one on one with each of our students. It is impossible to unpack the baggage that each student brings with them on their educational journey. Frankly, many of our students enter our classrooms with emotional baggage that may be hard to wrap our minds around, but it is important that those students know they have a champion.

Rita Pierson's dynamic **TED Talk** admonishes us to be that champion for students. To be that adult who will not give up and who will push students to reach their fullest potential.

There is a child in your class, there has been a child in your class, there will be a child in your class who is carrying the weight of the world on his or her shoulders. You do not have to save the world, but you have been placed in that classroom to help save that student.

- Tap into his or her interests.
- Let them know that you care.
- Let them know that you believe in them.

When they see that—great success will await them.

Doses of Grace:

> "Instruct the wise and they will be wiser still; teach the righteous and they will add to their learning" **(Proverbs 9:9, NIV)**.

> "I will instruct you and teach you in the way you should go; I will counsel you with my loving eye on you" **(Psalm 32:8, NIV)**.

> "In the same way, encourage the young men to live wisely. And you yourself must be an example to them by doing good works of every kind. Let everything you do reflect the integrity and seriousness of your teaching. Teach the truth so that your teaching can't be criticized" **(Titus 2:7-8, NIV)**.

Prayer:

God give me the grace to build lasting and impactful relationships with my students. Help me to push them beyond their preconceived notions and self-imposed limitations. Grant me the grace to be authentically me—the best me that I can be. Amen.

The Grace to know Your Why

"What is your why?"

I was attending a professional development session the first time I heard this question. As I looked at the question mark that dominated the PowerPoint slide, I quietly pondered the things that make me tick.

What deeply motivates and inspires me to teach?

On the first day of kindergarten, Mrs. Betty Davis instructed her eager little ones to draw a picture of the person they wanted to be when they grew up. Her assistant, Ms. Jean, provided us with the crayons and the largest pieces of construction paper I had ever seen. These supplies were necessary in order for us to complete our masterpieces.

I drew a lady wearing a vibrant green dress, bright red lipstick, cat eye glasses, with her hair styled in a bun. This was my visual representation of a teacher.

When I was asked why I drew a teacher, I simply stated that I wanted to help people.

I have never veered from that dream, neither have I regretted entering this field.

Students, co-workers, parents, and even administrators have wounded my heart over the years, but I have never lost my desire to help people. Daily I desire to make a positive impact in the lives of others.

Today, I am several decades older than the five year old sitting on the floor in College Street Elementary School, but anytime I question my "why," I can always travel to that place in time and feel the same zeal and passion I felt then.

I have not changed the world as I once believed I would, but when I visit the contents of my "Warm and Fuzzy" folder, I know that my journey has not been in vain.

My file cabinet has one manila folder with notes from former students, administrators, and peers. The contents of this folder always evoke an emotional response from me and allow me to reflect on positive moments from my career. I visit this folder when I need a reminder of why I do what I do.

Why do you teach?

There will be days when you may not feel appreciated, but appreciation should not be your why.

There will be days when you will feel like you are drowning in an ocean of paperwork but filling out forms is not your why.

There will be days when you will feel more motivated than your students, but your emotions are not your why.

You are called to teach.

You are called to make a difference in the life of a child. Somewhere there is a former student who would not be the person he is without your influence.

Beyond the lesson planning, formative assessments, data notebooks, and… there is a student who needs you to remember why you are leading the class. This student needs to know that if no one else believes in her, you do.

Your why is what drives you to do what you do. Do not forget your why—today's students need it.

Reflection:

When did you know you wanted to become a teacher?

Who were the teachers who made a positive impact on your life? Do you emulate anything about them?

Is there a moment that causes you to feel the zeal that you once did as a new educator? Do you have a "Warm and Fuzzy" notebook or folder to hold sentimental trinkets from your teaching career? If so, take a moment today and read a note from that file so your spark can be re-ignited.

Doses of Grace:

"A man's mind plans his way, but the Lord directs his steps and makes them sure" **(Proverbs 16:9, AMP).**

"For I know the thoughts and plans that I have for you, says the Lord, thoughts and plans for welfare and peace and not for evil, to give you hope in your final outcome. Then you will call upon Me, and you will come and pray to Me, and I will hear and heed you. Then you will seek Me, inquire for, and require Me [as a vital necessity] and find Me when you search for Me with all your heart" **(Jeremiah 29:11-13, AMP).**

Prayer:

Lord, forgive me for the times I have become so frustrated in this profession that I forgot that You ordained me to be here. Forgive me for not realizing that just as You have been patient with me, I also must be patient with others. I thank You for the grace You have shown toward me and it is with thanksgiving and gratitude that I show that same grace to others. I ask that You will allow the gift of teaching to be stirred up within me so I can begin again. My new beginning is today and I will treat each day as a precious gift from You. You ordained me to be here and I will continue to impart wisdom into the lives of those who have been entrusted to my care. I will make a difference in my students' lives because someone made a difference in mine. Amen.

Grace for What Matters Most

As an academic coach, I spend most of my time working one-on-one with adults, but that does not prevent me from being available to hear and respond to the requests of the most important stakeholders in the educational arena—the students.

Imagine my surprise when a student walked into my office one afternoon following my visit to his math classroom. The student was sitting with his head down during the 20 minutes I was completing my coaching cycle with his teacher. The teacher, knowing our area of focus was her lesson delivery, walked over to his desk several times and attempted to get the student involved in the lesson. Unfortunately, none of her attempts were successful.

The student sat across from my desk to share one vital piece of information. He wanted me to know that he was not "that student."

While I listened to Jacob discuss his desire to be successful in his class, he spoke at great length about the moment that he gave up. The words that resonated in my heart were that he gave up. His conversation was laced with all of the alternatives to school that he could think of. Here was this bright young man who was considering dropping out because he was being perceived as "that student."

I could have taken him on a tangent and shared my college experience with him, but instead I listened. I listened until he mentioned the teacher who had not given up on him. He spoke of his English teacher and everything about her and her class was positive.

He did not indicate that English was his favorite subject, but he knew that his English teacher genuinely cared about him.

I once entered a school and in every classroom the following quote by Forest Witcraft was prominently displayed on a wall:

"A hundred years from now it will not matter what my bank account was, the sort of house I lived in, or the kind of car I drove... but the world may be different because I was important in the life of a child."

The poster was not only indicative of the culture of the school, but also a constant reminder of the impact of our legacies as teachers.

Every student that enters our classroom deserves to be treated with love, compassion, and respect. Our students know if we care or if we are just going through the motions of teaching. The accolades of men will one day cease, but the impact that we have on the lives of our students will continue long after they walk out of our classrooms.

Be that teacher who cares.

Be that teacher who understands and shows what matters most.

Doses of Grace:

"If I speak with the tongues of men and of angels, but have not [a]love [for others growing out of God's love for me], then I have become only a noisy gong or a clanging cymbal [just an annoying distraction]" **(1 Corinthians 13:1, AMP).**

"May the favor of the Lord our God rest on us; establish the work of our hands for us-yes, establish the work of our hands" **(Psalm 90:17, NIV).**

"Therefore, my beloved brothers and sisters, be steadfast, immovable, always excelling in the work of the Lord [always doing your best and doing more than is needed], being *continually* aware that your labor [even to the point of exhaustion] in the Lord is not futile *nor* wasted [it is never without purpose]" **(1 Cor. 15:58, AMP).**

Prayer:

Lord, help me to fix my eyes on the things that please You. I understand that there are things that often outweigh what I feel is important, so show me what matters most to You so that I will please You daily. Help me to be an example to my students, my peers, and even my supervisors as I work daily to show students that I care. Give me the grace needed to create an atmosphere that will empower my students to be successful citizens who will make a positive impact on society. I recommit my life to service as I seek to honor You. Amen.

Abundant Grace

It is my prayer that this e-book has been a blessing to you. Prior to finishing this project, I had second thoughts about whether it would be a beneficial endeavor. As I prayed about completing this task, something transpired that allowed me to see the lasting impact teachers have on their students.

In the fall of 2017, one of my former co-workers passed away. Although he had over thirty years of teaching experience, my time working with him was very brief. I was moved to tears as I sat in his memorial service surrounded by students whose lives had been impacted by one teacher.

There are days when we feel overlooked, overworked, and overwhelmed, but I hope you have been encouraged to no longer focus on the negative components of our job. I pray you will give your best to your students because your work matters. The church was filled with those who had been his students during the past three decades. There were heads of grey who were probably taught algebra, geometry, and calculus with limited use of a calculator sitting beside the most regally coifed and dreadlock styled who had been educated under the Common Core umbrella with Math I, II, and III. There had been major shifts in education during his time as an educator and although the students in the church were from different walks of life, different races, and assuredly different religious backgrounds, they were all assembled in one place for one purpose—to show gratitude and respect to one man, their teacher.

Their teacher had made a positive impact in their lives.

When I left the service my heart was heavy because of the loss of a co-worker and friend, but I also had a nagging thought…when I transition, will I be remembered for the positive impact I had on the lives of my students.

The next day, I traveled to my hometown to celebrate my mother's birthday. My mind was no longer focused on the events of the previous day, I was just enjoying the opportunity to fellowship with my parents, my siblings, and our spouses and children.

God chose to use the moment I stepped to the salad bar as the moment to settle my mind concerning my earlier question.

A former student was also having lunch there with her family and when she saw me she came over to thank me for making a difference in her life.

I had not seen her in many years and had no idea that she had entered the field of education. I pray that what she said to me will remain in my mind for many years to come.

"Every day I walk into my classroom I know I am taking you and the lessons you taught me in that classroom with me. You were one of my favorite teachers."

I walked back to join my family with a heart of thanksgiving because I had asked God the day before if I had made an impact on the lives of others. And less than 24 hours later He sent ⁺Kristie to let me know me that I had.

It is my prayer that you will always encounter a Kristie. A student who will encourage you and motivate you on your lowest day. A student who will remind you that you are the reason they entered education, or you're the reason they are successful on whatever career path they have chosen. It is my prayer that when you need it the most, God will send a Kristie to you to show you His abundant grace.

I pray that He will continue to give you the grace to be the best educator you can be. There are so many students who are depending on you. We will not always know the students we have touched and we may not always see the fruits of our labor, but it is important for us to know that somewhere there is a child who is successful because of the grace you showed them.

As you complete this book, I want to share my prayer for you:

May you always be encouraged to do the work you have been called to do. I pray you will always be empowered to make a difference and a lasting impact on the lives of those you encounter. May God give you the grace to enlighten young minds and challenge them to be all they were created to be. May your classroom be a place of peace and tranquility. May His joy give you strength throughout each day. May His grace sustain you during difficult times and comfort you during times of despair. When you are frustrated and facing times of change, may His grace settle you. May you be overshadowed with His love and His grace—forever.

Amen.

A Final Note

I thank God for calling me into this profession. There are times when I feel unappreciated, but God always sends gentle reminders of the lasting impact I am making in the lives of my students. I continually seek His approval and guidance as I move the children and young adults toward a greater destiny than the one I can see today.

I appreciate His grace that empowers me to do more than I could have ever imagined. His grace sustains me during times of trials. His grace comforts me during times of despair. His grace settles me during times of change. I am so thankful for God's grace. If you are not acquainted with God and know that you need this grace in your life, won't you seek Him and ask for a daily dose of His grace? He loves you and wants to have a relationship with you. Just ask, He is more than willing to be your personal God.

Thank you for choosing to read this book. I pray it will be an empowering, encouraging, and enlightening read for you. Please subscribe to my email list at: IrisPBryant.com and keep in touch!

Join me on Social Media:

@irispbryant

If you enjoyed this book, it would be a tremendous blessing if you would leave a quick review on Amazon and Goodreads or share this book with others.

About the Author

IRIS PETERSON BRYANT is an educator, psalmist, author, and minister.

Iris earned a bachelor's from Fayetteville State University in English Education and is currently continuing her education at the University of North Carolina at Greensboro. She provides her insights through her blog and podcast at IrisPBryant.com.

During her educational career, which spans twenty years, she has taught students in grades 7-12, and currently serves as an academic coach and lead mentor.

She serves in the ministry of Love & Faith Christian Fellowship, Greensboro, NC and regularly speaks at conferences, events, and workshops sponsored by churches, schools, and educational organizations.

She and her husband David are the proud parents of four children.

www.ingramcontent.com/pod-product-compliance
Lightning Source LLC
Chambersburg PA
CBHW031217090426
42736CB00009B/962